*Whoosh!*

A train goes by.

It goes fast!

# Trains run on **tracks**.

# KINGFISHER READERS

level 1

# Trains

Thea Feldman

KINGFISHER
NEW YORK

**KINGFISHER**
LONDON & NEW YORK

Copyright © Kingfisher 2012
Published in the United States by Kingfisher,
175 Fifth Ave., New York, NY 10010
Kingfisher is an imprint of Macmillan Children's Books, London.
All rights reserved.

Distributed in the U.S. and Canada by Macmillan,
175 Fifth Ave., New York, NY 10010

Library of Congress Cataloging-in-Publication data
has been applied for.

Series editor: Thea Feldman
Literacy consultant: Ellie Costa, Bank St. College, New York

ISBN: 978-0-7534-6752-7 (HB)
ISBN: 978-0-7534-6753-4 (PB)

Kingfisher books are available for special promotions
and premiums. For details contact: Special Markets
Department, Macmillan, 175 Fifth Ave.,
New York, NY 10010.

For more information, please visit
www.kingfisherbooks.com

Printed in China
9 8 7 6 5 4 3 2 1
1TR/1011/WKT/UNTD/105MA

Picture credits
The Publisher would like to thank the following for permission to reproduce their material.
Every care has been taken to trace copyright holders. However, if there have been unintentional
omissions or failure to trace copyright holders, we apologize and will, if informed, endeavor
to make corrections in any future edition.
Top = t; Bottom = b; Center = c; Left = l; Right = r
Cover Shutterstock/Mark Oleksiy; Pages 3 Shutterstock/Mark Oleksiy; 4t Shutterstock/Allison
Achauer; 4–5 Shutterstock/Niv Koren; 6–7 Photolibrary/Age footstock; 8–9 Shutterstock/
Image Focus; 10–11 Shutterstock/tovovan; 12–13 Shutterstock/dusko; 14 Corbis/Jon Arnold/
JAI; 15 Kingfisher Artbank; 16t Shutterstock/14lcocl2; 16b Shutterstock/Henk Bentlage; 17
Shutterstock/Mikhail Zahranichny; 18t Shutterstock/Binkski; 18b Shutterstock/Brad Sauter; 19t
Shutterstock/s_oleg; 19b Corbis/Colin Garrett/Mile 92.5; 20 Photolibrary/Robert Harding Travel;
21 Shutterstock/gabczi; 22–23 Shutterstock/Avalon642; 22b Shutterstock/BartlomiejMagierowski;
23b Photolibrary/Imagebroker; 24 Corbis/Alen MacWeeney; 25 Corbis/Nick North; 26–27 Corbis/
B.S.P.I; 28 Photolibrary/Imagestate; 29 Corbis/Joseph Sohm; 30 Shutterstock/Pavel Losevsky;
31 Photolibrary/Transtock.

A train can go
anywhere there are tracks.

A train can go
across the desert.

A train can go
through a mountain.

A train can go over a bridge.

A train can go into a tunnel.

A train can go
under the ground.

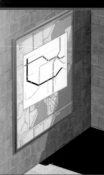

It can travel under city streets.

*Rumble, rumble!*

A train is coming.

Its wheels turn very fast on the tracks.

Then the wheels turn slower and slower.

The train slows down.

Then the wheels stop.

The train is here!

# What does a train carry?

It can carry boxes.

It can carry **coal**.

It can carry oil.

It can carry mail.

A train can carry people.

It can take them far from home.

# A train can have many **cars**.

car

Some cars are where people sit.

Other cars are where people can eat.

Some trains have cars where people can sleep.

Could you sleep on a moving train?

Every train has an **engine**.

The engine makes
the train move.

The engine is in
the first car of the train.

That car is called the
**locomotive.**

The **engineer** rides in the locomotive.

He drives the train.

A **conductor** rides in the cars.

He takes tickets and tells people where the train will stop next.

*Whoosh!*

Would you like to
take a train ride?

# Glossary

**cars** the parts of a train that carry things and people

**coal** a kind of rock that is burned to make heat or power

**conductor** the person on a train who takes tickets and tells people where the train will stop next

**engine** a machine that makes a train move

**engineer** the person who drives a train

**locomotive** the first car of the train, where the engine and engineer are

**tracks** the path a train runs on, made of metal rails and wood